The authoress was born in Jamaica and is of German nationality. At a very tender age, she was often mesmerised by literature: particularly those great, inventive, passionate poets, past and present, who have mastered the art of personification.

The love of the countryside provided her with immense, visionary liberty; the freedom to explore and expand was not foreign to her. The wisdom of the classical music masters and philosophers gave her an excuse to waltz away to her individuality. She also believes in the true, rebellious, wild recklessness of love and nature.

She came to live in Germany and England in the 1980s, acquiring a Diploma in Business Studies. Whilst living in Germany, she worked in the theatre in a production of *Kabale und Liebe* by Friedrich Schiller. She has also indulged herself in the world of fashion over many years.

She has travelled extensively. Her love for the south of Europe led her to live in the Principality of Monaco. Since her return to England, she has worked in education.

GRÄFIN

String of Pearls

Diverse Poetry

AUSTIN MACAULEY PUBLISHERS™
LONDON · CAMBRIDGE · NEW YORK · SHARJAH

Copyright © Gräfin (Marie Daley von Huth) 2023

The right of Gräfin (Marie Daley von Huth) to be identified as author of this work has been asserted in accordance with section 77 and 78 of the Copyright, Designs and Patents Act 1988.

All rights reserved. No part of this publication may be reproduced, stored in a retrieval system, or transmitted in any form or by any means, electronic, mechanical, photocopying, recording, or otherwise, without the prior permission of the publishers.

Any person who commits any unauthorised act in relation to this publication may be liable to criminal prosecution and civil claims for damages.

A CIP catalogue record for this title is available from the British Library.

ISBN 9781398486782 (Paperback)
ISBN 9781398486799 (e-pub e-book)

www.austinmacauley.com

First Published 2023
Austin Macauley Publishers Ltd®
1 Canada Square
Canary Wharf
London
E14 5AA

Dedication

My Prof.

The intellectual – unforgettable "FRIENDSHIP"

I am

Acknowledgements

My daughter Sydney Roya and her spouse (better than her best) Anton Dementiev, for a quick brain-storm and their support

Preface

This *String of Pearls* is formed to take you back to the past, to stand gloriously in the present and display keen loyalty to the future yet unknown.

A collection of old-world, new-world, sanctioned charm, which will not fade and vanish as time passes, but will be upheld in a rarer shade that will withstand and span many lifetimes.

The authoress has not pursued rhyming stanzas in her work, but concentrated on "free verses" to bring about the true colour of randomness, in thoughts that fall smoothly on the heart's chambers, to bring about exquisiteness to the reader and listener alike.

An unannounced thrill to the spirit, almost whimsical in manner, similar to the saying: "A fish can see the bait but not the hook, until..."

A great authoress you will meet; your time will be well spent, and you will repeatedly seek and claim her words as your own.

Indelible are the ones that uplift and console you in a righteous, desperate hour when you answer the call to read them one by one, like a *string of pearls*.

Poems

4 am	10
After the Rain	11
Autumn	12
Camellia	13
Childhood Tales	14
Choice	15
Daffodils	16
Dawn	17
Eve	18
Farewell	19
Friendship	20
Garden	21
Goodbye	22
Happiness	23
He	24
Horse	25
If I Must	26
Intuition	27
Lament	28
Late Morning	29
Life	30
Love in a Mist	32
Love oh Love	33
Love	34
A Moment in Time	35
Moon	36
The Night	37
Old	38
Opera / Concert	40
Rainy Day	41
Roses	42

The Shore	43
Silence	44
Snow Scene	45
Solitude	47
Summer	48
Thoughts	50
Time	52
Waterfall	53
Wild	54
A Winter's Noon	55

4 am

A prayer whispered,
Long linger the bucolic sounds and scenes of late dusk,
Then deafening silence,
Sleep overwhelms me, deep, wholesome,
Visions of a dream dominate the spirited mind.

Soon to peel away the divine-like stillness:
Tunes of yesterday replay,
Flood with chords that plague,
Imprison and twist the mind.

Toss, turn weary,
Weave into a net bigger and bigger, deeper and deeper,
Clawing at the very pit, poking edges of thoughts,
Darkness overpowers, thick gloom shows no face.

In wee-hours sleep press pillow,
Deep slumber conquers, as if under a spell cast;
Not a movement, not a turn,
Such tranquil bliss!

Alas! haunting outbursts of wild birds soak early crystal air,
Disturbing a sovereign soul,
Dawn's grey shade heeds to the romance of the rising sun,
Elbow subtle into pure heart of first light.

4 am disappears quickly as it came,
A creeping sound – not even heard.
Full glories of daybreak take shape,
Begin.

After the Rain

Last rain of summer unspoilt, I knew you would come,
Mingling with heavy giving clouds you call,
Leaving damp, dusky odour of Petrichor.
Potpourri, woody, breaks through the nostrils,
Perfectly dotted with pungent perfume.

Warm rising air, one by one buds hang heads low,
The last of the wild crimson roses, hang on trail still,
Loll into the split bitter fresh aroma you spray.
Taut light warm soft raindrops, flowing in their veins,
Bequeathed by the giving drops, compact on the pregnant earth.

A comforting call of a wild bird nearby,
Perched on a vertical wispy vine,
Coupled by lonely tweets from the robin redbreast;
Now earth awakes, straightens, replenishes,
Filled with raking worms from the giving ground.

Gone now are the flaccid moments,
Dry limbs, cracked barks, parched no more.
Ferns, ivy all alike, swim in the pattern of heavy droplets,
The myrtle face – glad, clapping its leaves in last refreshing drop,
Tightly closing its eyes in the quickest of winks.

All on earth's plain stand erect with beauty, purpose call,
Together anchored by the quiet touch of gleaming raindrops.
Childhood tales of rain forever, scar with moist mildew memories,
Summer's heat a memory now,
As gradual silence of its rain miscarries, then hush!

Autumn

Pearl bundles of light behind window panes,
As summer waltzed away with its warming rays,
Enticing me to hang on short languid afternoons;
I watch the grey hours rapidly unfold.

Grave-like silence doth call, wrapping its claws in mid-air,
Broken – flapping wings in thicket heard,
Surrendering to and fro, then quiet murmur,
No bird doth sing alone, the swallow its last song!

Yet, the autumn silence served a warning,
The nearby shrub weeps, as in non-composing company,
Compelling the noon air to loosen its quiet grip!
Ah! there she hung, harnessed in the swing of autumn.

Tone set aflame, stitched together,
The shadow o'er it lay, set, weakened by the autumn hours,
The weeping wind rage unyieldingly, dictates the pattern to follow,
Seduced not by the still, cunning silence.

Soon mankind and creature in exile be,
Longing for the warm days gone by,
No doubt spell-binding memories,
Underneath deep-sea blue willing skies.

Gone now is the scent of blossoms that once filled the morning air,
Birds that sang, visited often in flocks, grow now weary,
Grand green flourishing carpet shone no more,
And the trees that once housed the honey-suckle looked sparse, bare.

Now the heavens resound, thick clouds gather, coast to coast shows no pardon,
Wild brawling wind cast its cry, as if to say goodbye,
The pompous days of summer shook, changed hands,
Then like a faded rose, lost in time.

Camellia

I see you in clusters white, delicate pink,
Hush by winter passing by.
Soon feathery snow will kiss your brow,
Under first gentle, soft burst of its kind,
White and pink petals push through,
Below stubby branches and evergreen leaves,
Where summer birds their beds once made,
Now, ceased by robins to hide from their nosy prey.
Oh! snowflakes on your tender tips,
Gleaming, like precious gemstone in dry bitter cold,
As night falls beneath the spangled sky you shine.
White camellia embosoms a lonely robin,
With its puffed orange chest,
Flitters from branch to branch,
Blanketed by the cold frosty air,
Beneath a safe haven seeks,
A spell of radiance – no doubt cast.
Never mind, sweet robin dear,
I will wrap you ever so tight,
Your wings, no need for flight,
You and I will rest till winter – late.

Childhood Tales

Sweet rain of youth,
Ever so fleeting,
Minds too young, purity of soul.

Innocent laughter fill fields near,
Companion of vast green cornfields,
With their ears of corn stood proud,
Hair stringy, long, yellow.

Pattering footsteps on hard parched earth,
Stomping, wading, slashing through sharp blades of corn young,
Create a symphony, a sharp melody: to the otherwise still noon.

Crickets seem to have hymn sheets,
Belting high-pitched notes unabashedly in the wind's tale.
The resounding notes of alto and contralto invite nosy grasshoppers,
Adding their lofty tunes, melting the rough uneven plain.

Wild grass on the prairie lends bed to olive faces,
The determined deep-orange sun pierces the pure blue sky,
Ears closely press to earth.
The underground spring had its song too,
And compels to wade.

Slowly, nature's evening sun begins to fade,
The golden dust of childhood tales flicker,
Like the countless diamonds of the starry night skies,
As life coaxes all: as a master into its winding light.

Choice

Oft I dream of a choice:
Never know all, but a few I do,
When to bet, when to spew.
My wanton mind doth wander,
Through the garden of choice it swims,
Ploughing, paying life's bulky penance.
But I confess, the later more agreeable,
With not much worth, I came to buy,
Lends small justice, no doubt,
With presence makes a heart much lighter,
Lurking beneath a bittersweet harvest,
Bearing witness of a martyr of choice doth prove.
Ponder choice, ponder well,
Rewards make in a giving soul,
Burst of laughter or that of sorrow,
Sweet wounds more often weeps,
The joy that captures the soul,
Choice filled the air with life's fragrance perfume,
While the stars kindle your desire, clothe in anticipation.
Deceiving world, I said "Alas",
Left me unwilling to pay life's hefty price of choice.

Daffodils

Your shaking buds, vibrant blooms,
Shades of nature's pallet, finest yellow,
Soft, deep, delicate, emerge from your womb,
Beheld by naked eyes, soft and mellow.

How could you still be so perfect?
Even though rough, chilly winds of April cast to and fro,
Pray tell your precious secret, lest you forget!
Before the wilder winds toss you in an endless blow!

Do you ever grow weary and faithless?
A feeling to forsake your constant duty?
"Answer me", whisper, tell me softly you are ageless,
Like the sweet tones of some long-gone Debussy.

I see you in clusters bloom,
Withstanding the harsh blunt of late winter,
Tell me, your secret forever entomb,
Nod your head in the subtle wind, kiss her.

Petals ever so perfect,
Let me count, yes, six I think,
No, not one left without being checked.
If this was Egypt, I would name you Sphinx.
Oh, now I know your secret!
It is in the long thin stem,
That bends almost into a deep net.
I will now sing your praise in solemness,
And eagerly await you next spring.

Dawn

Dawn appears with soft flickering light,
Encrusted with promises of a new day,
Filled with symphony of chirping,
Engulfs and lightens the morning air,

The moments stretch their eager hands,
Filled with glorious anticipation.
I reach out, embrace,
And feel light with happiness.

Eve

It came,
Cast its shadow upon the land,
Bewitching everything that's light,
Enslaving all creatures into deep slumber.

The hours passed,
Its shade grows thin and pale,
Suddenly, the faithful aged sun
Moves over the horizon,
Conquered by its dark prey night.

Farewell

To my faded friend, farewell, farewell,
Your change is here to see.
I'm left to walk the lonely path without your company,
A path the wise and brave dare take.

I recall the shining sun, mornings grey disappear,
The downpour of the rain,
I linger and watch the rare shades of the rainbow,
Transfixed, till the evening light turns into a full moon.

Time shows no error, time shows no sign,
The days now grow longer, the hours linger,
No tears shed, no pain felt,
But left behind sweet memories still.

Friendship

Eyes close in balmy afternoon sun,
Spilling thoughts of friendship behind mind's eye,
Like splitting rays of diamonds light and soft:
Oh, such a soothing thought!

Delicious ripe fruit of lingering friends,
Some took years, some shorter,
Yet, viewed in eyes the same; sacred, true, faithful,
The abiding sweetness of the years.

Unforced, not falsely fettered or shackled,
Nor through a sieve strained,
Its contents abide deep in virtue,
No blemish or strife.

Though years may change thee,
As leaves from autumn trees depart,
Thy fibre of strength lolls still, weathering tough storms,
Delicate, yet strong, as that of a spider's silken woven thread.

No fire fan, no water pour, but lend a love,
Morph in that of the Greeks, Alexander and Hephaestion, festooned with sacredness.
A purity of soul, pass through the gateways to caress the hems of the gods,
A religious bond, wrapped in pilgrimage of spirit.

Bosom, packed and filled with peace,
Ignites a divinity, and echoes a call of noble minds.
Oh listen! Yes, listen, if such rare shade unfolds on thy path,
Then say, thou hath moved unseen hearts of moon and stars alike.

Garden

Like a queen you shine your comeliness,
A rare type, enchantress, leaves speechless,
A sweet chapter of beauty bright, captured by the afternoon sun,
Entices, arrests, and lightens the willing heart.
Weeds cash in on your beguiling beauty; you hide your secret well,
Mapped by rows of flowers all gay and bright,
Lilies, roses, hibiscus, take charge, parading oh! their wooing prettiness.
Your sweet crop, milked by bees, hummingbirds, butterflies alike,
Gathered to hum away in the languid afternoon tea-time delight,
As orioles, with fine wings rapidly beating nearby,
Barge during the sermon, partaking in sweet drinks of hibiscus, wage no war,
Together, drink, fill their guts with sticky juice in the smouldering heat.
Dragonflies with wings of fine art in unison hear,
Their sounds pad the inviting fragrant air,
Dance, shine, devoted sapphire light, fierce, beautiful,
Crowned by brimming insects unknown, state a-glow.
Glorious garden, swaying to melody of brushing winds, flapping of wings,
Now, autumn rain your captor, awaits, soon – drop by,
Sadly fill your heart with tears,
Autumn lends, if ever, no justice fair.

Goodbye

Little sweetness in parting, I was told,
Yet the heart must stay bold,
Through many an hour unfold,
And the spirit often goes cold.

Oh! what sweet bitter refrain,
That goes and comes again,
With much pain a long road, no gain,
The mind commands to remain sane.

The wind of time doth steady its sting,
They all are that magical thing,
If only I could grow one single wing,
That has a mighty wild cling.

Like a bird we must fly on ahead,
Alone often on the soft side of the bed,
With the dull pain throbbing in the head,
Dare not the weak tears fed.

Curse not the lonely moment of sorrow,
There will be kinder ones tomorrow,
Though on your forehead sunken deep fine furrow,
Leap for joy, knowing they're only a short-time burrow.

Rest, not at all heart stay broken,
A song in the soul can be a glorious token,
Though love leave a mind with its bitter sweet portion unspoken,
Take a deep breath, your doom is not yet spoken.

Happiness

It's a divine flame,
Impossible to tame,
It probably drives you insane.
Fan it,
Keep it alive,
'Tis your ultimate guide,
A compass to survive through life's rusty slide.
Thou willst fly with winds unseen,
Then learn to glide...

He

He, of a man, comely, distinguished, wise,
Wrapped in leaves of destiny and fate,
Command my heart, modest and true,
Curl in bliss for what it's worth,
And tame the heart, as solitude can.

A face: warm, enticing, bashful;
Lips that bend in a sweet smile, ready to play;
Eyes full of grace, ones that hide deep pain,
Yet lock in a quiet disdain;
Beard peppered, for nature surely has taken its toll.

A beguiling smile warms the heart at bay,
Kiss its chambers as lips upon a brow, soft and soothing.
Heart so soft and bending, no room for reproach unfair,
But nobly approve with sly refreshing candour.
Oh, oh what a man! the wild heart dare not tame!

He, of a man, brings sunshine unknown,
A smile that breaks upon unseen shore,
Disperse all the hidden gloom.
No need to say, too modest a man,
A fragment of imagination, yet not proven
He of a man.

Horse

It's trapped here:
Only way to catch it
Is to set it free,
Free to be king or queen,
And for the highest bidder befitted,
To fly with wings devoted,
Such a beautiful thing.
No one can know its mind,
Only a snake charmer one might say.
An almost placid creature in its wake,
A steady gaze, like a mighty one it stands,
True, fast in gait,
Loyal, a true-blue to the gallop.
Let you fly, let you feel free,
Take a flight, take a gambol,
With shiny outer-coat, dark,
Smooth like rich-old velvet,
Like well brewed Irish ale.
A god in no measure it hails,
Cocooned in natural elegance,
Neck more graceful than any swan.
If you choose, then you have chosen a good thing.

If I Must

If I must, head held high,
Statue, abide with dignity and pride,
If I must, back straight on my command,
I shall not bow nor lie,
Brave, strong, self-assured I stand.

Though pain and disappointment twist and rock my bones,
None shall my foe or raiment be.
If I must, hang on with all my might,
Face upright,
Till the shadows disappear,
By the redeeming light.

Intuition

Acquaint yourself, still soft voice,
Oh yes! such pearls of life must be fostered!
Sweet whisper of peace and silence: watches, moves non-committal,
Like a gateman chooses his visitors.

Lavish channels free miracles,
Advice pave, forge lead to golden murmur,
A voyage in head and heart,
A soft touch at your soul's portal.

It comes to defend and aid, in the shifting plates of life:
Wrap itself in a sheet, pure-white,
Heed to its sudden subtle warning,
Ebb and flow with purpose.

Intense attention to call that bid,
Hang onto the dishevelled enchanting words,
Clothe in light – epiphany, cloak in golden light!
Dance when the stars dance:
Dance when the stars dance: die as it nourishes the soul.

Lament

The air is soft and smooth, my soul doth cry soft tears,
Flushed with morning dew, momentum you gain,
Strangling my woes, intensifying my grief without mercy,
Now dark clouds gather, rent with rain.

Light as rain, dark as shadow,
You lead, compel me to follow with quiet footsteps,
My grief gallops, its bitterness disperses into my arid soul,
All heaven falls at my feet in the late morning hour.

My inner being rampages with rage, hurries with confusion,
As my lament breaks upon its shore, crashes against the crevices of my fragile heart,
Carried upon the waves of betrayal, like a shadow faint,
Loss, lashes, cries of relentless bitter tears.

Oh soul! I beseech you to bear me gladness,
Beat your bright light in my dull, dark, arid soul,
Defend me with your sweet voice,
Let your divinity hasten without vanity.

When nightfall, grant my soul its light with pale shade,
Lavish me with heaven lacquer under starry skies,
Brand me with reappearing hope, diminishing disappear,
A hope with intent of abiding constancy, to lament no more.

Rip my pain, the lament which dethroned me most,
Sacrifice the moment, replace its keen inspiration,
With the symbol of love under the crescent moon,
Abide and fix my soul, permit me to lament no more.

Late Morning

Images of sun exploded, sprawled its light,
Enveloped mixed sky, entwined with broad seeds of soothing wretched winds
Resting upon hues filtering through:
Like an earthly king sitting upon his throne in pomp-grandeur,
Dispersing its weak meagre warmth, provoking a stir on soft earth.

The carpet of full green blinked with nonchalance,
Unperturbed by the invasion of frivolity,
Knowing this stage is short-lived, shows an effortlessly forced glistening blink.
Amidst, human souls impulsively succumb in obedience – rejoice in eagerness.
Willing to hold on with tenacity, failed to be perturbed by this fleeting thrill.

Quick jolt of reality reappears, leaving all beneath a vast space of quiet light.
The green bed beneath blade with tips of light, stood on guard in full alignment,
Stood upright,
Without wind,
Without duty,
Without purpose.

Life

Life sends and lends its constellation,
Sets through shared space,
A chronicle unleashes the desire,
Openly drags along at a constant pace,
Behoves us to join freely in the yet unknown.

Submit to its fair glories,
A sweet melody it holds,
Filled with hopes and dreams, like flower's tight bud before unravelling,
And dreams of days to display their beauty.
Take from its outstretched palm; in not too long a time this will end.

Labour with love, false heart-broken vows,
What shades do you bear?
The heart and mind take rip,
Like daily slaves, carried with much disdain,
Oh! not to switch the disappointment with pain.

Real joys seldom prove, timely setbacks linger in droves,
Look back and tremble at life's delights,
Think! not all in vain, tarry not towards the light,
But put up a brave enduring fight,
For that, you'll suck the sweet juice that floods and bursts.

Sincere laughter that warms the given heart
Transcends its soft, smooth silken charmed hours;
Prisoners of fleeting moments, subdued, bewitched,
Drink in its tick, if only short and sweet like sugar-plum,
For that too is only coated with time.

A valley of a thousand miles, harvest is at hand,
Life entwines with rebellious thoughts,
Notes are few, yet a full choir beckons singing lines of hope,
As swallows their last song sing
Of long summers lost; winter approaches, life marches on.

Sorrow moments grey, life, love, fear shrinks beneath,
And night's sleep casts no light, but dimming shadow,
Torments, rivals, pangs of labour,
Defeat endures, no sight of hope,
But writhe thoughts in kingly state,
Life leads us to its bidding!

Plead the scar, whispering on life's wind,
Its delight wrapped in harsh melody,
A timely echo lends a bleak bitter symphony.
As a clock chimes at the appointed hour,
Life disappears without a trace, with all its pomp and glorious promises.

Love in a Mist

A waltz with a flower in the cold morning mist,
Enchanted by its feathery charm,
Carried, lost footing into endless desire,
Of notes, cool, ill-shaped splendour.

Dampness lurks in the shadow,
Romance by the hour,
Beckons to indulge in a day unknown, without promise,
Harkens to call, harken to its seductive drum of pacific blue pompous allure.

Linger yet, soak up the haunting opus of nature's endless beauty,
Cocoon in a star, spell-bound, bewitching.
Sunrise bids toil to open its dewed petals,
Before the glories spin nothingness, steals its heart: loss in the hours.

Destined to die, then disappearing like a shard of a dream,
Embraced by the soft white light,
Never to return,
Unless commanded by the magic of time.

Love oh Love

Like a Viking on an unknown sea,
I savour the thrill of thee:
Savagely, tumultuously you entered – poise – a soft light,
The jaunty emotion was pure delight,
I couldn't resist such a frisky plight.

Oh love thy pleasing texture!
A tongue framed to music, a grand gesture.
Succumb to your bidding, like the passing of a poison chalice,
Captures, devours as by a golden morning, without malice,
Opening its arms to pay tribute to the new-born sound of T. Tallis.

Enchanting shivers of love,
A sweeter re-order from above,
Lost in sweet words, that of birds cling on heart,
Radiating raptures that cannot depart.
Like delicate potent scent of jasmine on late summer's eve, tenderness impart.

A pungent sweet delicacy that can entice and calm,
Bathes the soul with hints of nameless charm,
No fairer page could balm or set the soul aflame without alarm,
Yes, the river of love knows not whence its birth,
Yet leaves behind a whiff, wrapped tightly around the girth.

Love

Like a wretched beast you pounce into her heart,
Sit with ease, content,
Casting your shadow o'er her,
Scattering celestial rapture that soothes, arouses her inner torch.

A sense of endearment leaves powerless her heart,
A quiet vision, ray of bliss,
Like the approaching dawn:
Owning its glow with grace.

Oh love! oh love! don't let her go;
In the asking, she will gladly surrender with bliss.
Just beckon, just wait,
Lingering with glee, linger yet.

A Moment in Time

I pluck, drink the ripe fruit again and again,
And suck the poisoned nectar.
Drunk without – no fix – no antidote,
Gain fear this can't last.

Oh! not a care! too sweet to retreat,
Succumb to the passing moment,
A prisoner was surely born, you see,
Feasting upon the forbidden, too hard to let go.

A feast of bliss, half-truth given,
Even then, wise deep spirit disapproves.
Draw shades in the evening – note nothingness of day.
No regrets, no remorse! Such an array!

In the end this was given; hours gain,
Gratefulness, triple abundance, attended without woe.
A heart doth leap? Hours gain,
All tied up in a dream, a glorious dream.

Moon

You rise in the east, feeble, delicate, untouchable;
Born among stars, you gaze with your ghost-like feathery eyes,
Tucked betwixt clouds, disguised in its cloak.
Presence fickle softens the night sky;
Alone you send your sombre shadow, changing,
Mere mortals cast their eyes mesmerized.
Soft hues fall, earth's full: like a warning angel, in the night sky,
Your light serves to warm the bosom,
Melts the heart, sends it dreaming,
Then disappears, telling no tale of your warming light.
Again, nightfall approaches, slow and dark:
You show your face the same repeat,
With your soft feathery eyes' dull light.

The Night

Star locked, feathery room,
Peeping through tight bars,
Falling into faded glory.
A dark blanket cold, silent,
Sheathe the willing land.
The heavens lie lifeless,
Caught in a glory of dreams;
No joy to be heard nor felt,
No creatures to be seen, no, not one.
Darkness imprisons, chokes,
Yet no sound to be heard.
Black rain bellows at its side,
Pounding on my window pane.
A light now extinguishes,
Through the encircling mist.

Old

Slippers tattered – worn, threadbare:
Like the oriental rugs on floor with edges no more,
Days of splendour recall,
Bright, vibrant, youth empowered by order of hope and beauty.

Now I sit by the crackling fire,
Its flames of youth filled with vibrance, as if dancing around a maypole.
Roaring, unceasingly, it somehow lends a sinister warmth,
And graces a now deep-lined face.

The puppeted, menacing images play havoc,
Glistening, casting a shadow on peppered stringy hair:
Once was thick as a brush,
Lies lifelessly on a determined crown.

Grimaces of sun weave a brow,
Mind-sad heart caught in the thrust of passing love,
Some unrequited, tied mystery still, requited – call to thunderous spell.
Oh how reverent those fleeting years!
Hands frail, bones clothed in thin veiny skin,
Bespectacled eyes – now weak and watery,
Shuffling feet, sore and swollen:
Clasp in a frame too wiry – too frail.

Dusty books, pages worn – were white, now cream;
Paragraphs – chapters play over and over,
Left with contents that once thrilled, excited, engaged;
Now fragile, faint, out of grasp, clouded memory, laps into hopelessness.

Oh breath! a gust of air once filled with life,
Revert to slow, determined, calculated pause.
Gloom of darkness now murmurs, as fate beckons to fields of grey,
Yet clings to sweet thoughts, as gentle as lips landing upon a child's brow.

The autumn of life approaches stealthily on life's cobbled pavement,
Then gently slipping into its final stage.
The last crackle, the last flame, now fades with the dying embers.
Unafraid, I embrace all the memories still, watch them roll into the last moments,
Of eternal solitude.

Opera / Concert

Stucco captures the sight,
Grand tier, loggia, over-hanging balconies.
The splendour awaits:
An eager audience waits with bated breath.
Low murmuring, hum like voices,
Array of a rustle, little black dresses in equal movement, adds to its delight.
Shimmering, crystal studded gowns
Align with sharp-fitted tuxedo suits and smoking jackets.
Now, wild claps, relentless deafening applause,
Like raindrops on an uneven pavement.
Anticipation plays host to sudden obedience.
The orchestra belts succulent, cloying differing tones,
Almost, in flawless unison.
The Steinway and Sons play havoc with haunting:
Sweet, beguiling notes
Capture and evoke tales of passion.
The air comes ablaze with ripples of sound, resounding, warm,
Flutters, whispers, speaks and cleaves,
To willing hearts, compelling souls to weep,
Harkens to a tune lost, transporting to lands unknown.
Oh, such pleasing enchanting hair-raising melodies!
Flute, harp, oboe, trumpet shells' rhythm crisp,
Beckoning chords of rich music break in ebb and flow:
Yield to turbulent, magnificence of ivory – keys almost ghost-like,
Yet, peel – steady harmony of bitter-sweet.
The harvest of sprawling tones,
Like the warm whisper of butterflies' wings,
Skilfully showers in glorious euphony,
Captivating, faint-like charming rich refrain
Devours and uplifts limp spirits.
Heart-gripping tones rolled into jollity of tears,
As final arias mingle, minds rock with intense emotions,
Illumine the soul with utter delight.
Heaven moves, dies,
And leaves on earth's plain mortals,
To dine on its fragrance of glory,
And now, peeled chords perish, in bitter sweetness.

Rainy Day

Rain, Rain, Rain!
Torrents of white rain sprout! gush! level!
Crippling sunny thoughts of man and beast,
Relentless, spiralling droplets teem from east and west
As heaven's eyes weep – show no mercy.

Fierce, determined, full with misgivings – no sorrow,
Showering beads among turf, swiftly disappearing,
Acting as if land is burrowed,
Lashes and dances in the soft warm wind,
Till earth's plain sings no more its arid song.

Leaves, trees hung, heads low, as if their tears they hide,
Roses drunk no more – laden,
Fifty other flowers on bush bent,
As virgin petals utter soft tears of rain with droplets peeping,
Left to relish in death, untimely.

When dark shadows fall, bewitch me in love's stately hour,
Then my lament of thee will beat my heart with raging gladness.
Yet, strangle me not with your tears at daybreak,
Nor whisper too tenderly or wickedly to me,
For that alone is pure soothing vanity!

Rain, rain, tiptoe away, cease,
Take your feast, pomp and glory: heaven below cares no more,
To sink, seek nor sing your heavy Wagner-like refrain.
Let me learn of your downpour of tears,
Far, far away in distant skies.

Ah wretched rain! my summer is short – soon dies.
Let me be free, dry to pay homage to my warmer days,
As the dreaded, dull autumn days lurk in the shadows,
To imprison the sharp rays of my beloved sun.
So, tarry no more, sweet rain, tarry no more.

Roses

Through dark sod of winter long repose,
Hail their beauty! now strutting in warm summer's air,
Petals spark with morning dew burst,
Early sunrise shines its heavenly beams bright.

Set alight renewed comforts,
Whence a summer morning appear,
Trail your bloom, proud as a peacock,
Delicate scent scattered "Oh so near"!

Long green smooth stems tall,
Sweet buds do linger, steadfast unshaken,
Grandiose beauty lacks fear, shows daring,
Adorn among thorns protected and mighty.

Before-long sunken sun leaves its joy behind.
Linger now the clouds with rain,
To the late wild summer winds, you harken gush with glory-hail;
Your once green leaves, now defaced with blackened mould.

Not long, before autumn nears, then winter shows grim face,
As if mocking bestowed fate, petals droop and give their last winks.
Winter's bed now calls, silent as graves, hush and cold,
Roses, nevertheless, you leave behind sweet memories still.

The Shore

Oh! May a thousand years rise and salute!
No great trifle with wind you raise,
Lapping miraculous waves, join inviting hues of peach ashore,
Sending majestically scalloped corridors to play and dance,
Drawn into the haunting harp-like melody sweet trance,
Dashing and crashing as the willing shore abide hypnotize,
Succumb to your ebb and flood soft sand cling-rush,
Resounding to the rhythm like African drums a-beating.
Oh such an earthy sublime beauty and sound,
Lashing, splashing, slapping, silvery rich blue,
Foaming, in almost a rapturous tale in unison crash,
Caressing on soft awaiting pearl peachy sand,
Glistening shades of blue and white your edges show.
Perhaps orchestrated by the light of the harvest moon,
A kiss of blue from the heavens shines a turquoise wonder.
With splendour transform in floating magic ribbons,
Lively, intrigued and spread such peace and tranquillity,
Albeit, lie constant in the caressing of the demanding wind.
Oh! the never-ceasing wonder of you,
Hovering with your haunting thrill,
Leaving an echo, silently replaying in my heart.

Silence

A tightly woven net drawn across early summer's sky,
Bees hovered between fragrant flowerbeds
And roses held precious petals dear,
While thorns' points lay still, between their grasp.
Dare not to weep, but embrace the abiding silence.

Fields afar harbour glory in their soul in deep silence,
Trailing clouds leap and rush by,
Naked and unashamed hang their heads low,
Not a tone, not a word, not a woe,
Bound to the most heavenly place.

The soft sun clothes in its bright rays,
Dances and adorns the earth with its timely shades,
Harken to the silent whisper on soft winds,
Each corner of the earth opposes not such a quiet celestial voice,
But basks in its unseen presence in the shady breeze.

Soft silence that moves the wings of birds, let loose to fly,
Flooding stars that sparkle, dance, march into sweetness of the night,
Surrounding graves there lay still, long forgotten,
Full moon betray not in cowardness of duty,
But cast its spell with eerie-like brave known heroes.

I beckon thee my silence! Bequeath me with thy aura too,
Deny me not, hence my craved solitude has no end.
Lend me the silence that you have bestowed upon nature,
Shed your light in my deep soul, to you I owe my loyalty,
Soap me with your softness of random gust.

Silence me with uncharted peace and freedom,
Permit me thy glory to bask and abide,
With you my trust alone find,
Hush!

Snow Scene

Subdued under relentless, sacred crisp white flakes,
Evergreens stood firm, adjudge,
Guarded above by long, slender white bell-cap tips,
Unwilling to surrender into the heavy hands of falling snowflakes.

Wispy, blackberry bush, with thin vines,
Created a memory of long last summer,
With thorns weigh low now, as if in humility,
Left with no strength to fight.

Winter camellia embodies crowns of snow-heavy,
Exhibits still, constant proud pink blooms in defiance,
In clusters – undivided,
Looking on in pure delight.

Heavy snowed sky welcomes a flock of seagulls,
Blending wings in pure white, soft grey.
Moving clouds keep them at bay,
Their elegant wings flap in unison.

A riotous gust of savage wind showed no sign of mercy,
Hurled, loosened, divided leaves now compact in white thick fluff,
Into a tale of submission among white bough and twigs,
Careening softly to the ground.

Without halting,
Dancing noiseless flakes bow heads gracefully,
Inviting stillness, hastily spiral into accepting their fate,
On earth's thick feathery plain.

Winter's bountiful delight of berries,
From a holly bush in the distance,
Provide a backdrop of red, white contrast, ceaseless, unchanging,
Sparks of red tones as the bravest, protrude the crown of white, fragile settling chips.

Undeniable, winter's divinity proves itself true,
Beauty, oh beauty, you are everywhere!
Those who seek,
Bend to adhere.

Solitude

My solitude my sin, all chaos within,
You seep your way into my mind.
Burrow your roots in my deepest soul, making it thine:
Oppressing vexing light of spirit, hard to define,
Hurling in path an abyss, no time to align,
Without a slight landing in such wild design:
The darkness dividing my light entwines.

A fight! without shadow of prospect in sight,
Slow sadness coils around me, yet I must win,
You shan't conquer! I dare with all my might!
Grace of the gods, where shall I begin?
Revelation of spring, dull divinity in its wing.
A heart is led to sing,
Holding on the goal like a true knight.

The long summer days lurk in the shadows,
Beyond every cloud, promises of hope carry,
Soft, swift, jagged imperfect dance in the meadow,
Fair sight of consciousness tarries,
A cast dark soul to feed.

Lost in the moment lead,
A glimmer perfect connect,
Shook, cast a flight indeed:
I knew I had to win! the dark battle I must reject,
My fight of solitude, my sin.

Summer

Pungent, sweet deep scents
Tantalize the senses everywhere, make sense;
Hyacinth, lilies, flowers in bloom,
Vines green, strong, displaying a hearty plume.
Maturity wears daring, soon hardly any room,
No sign or thoughts of lurking doom.

Bees humming aloft in mid-air,
No care for their affair:
Wings that flicker, tinker like cymbals,
Setting off a wild, wanton-like tremble,
With the lingering monotony of counting symbols,
Where millions of similar breeds sacredly assemble.

Butterflies steadfastly alight their cocoons,
Tearing here and there without fear like a baboon,
Dancing, prancing as in a trance,
Basking in the sun, like in the south of France,
Showing no fear, to set off an avalanche,
Landing fiercely on any given high branch.

Blackbirds, robins, thrushes and twits emit a cacophony of deafening sounds,
Swiftly take flight, perhaps homebound,
A language in decibels deciphered,
Levels of joy carelessly measured,
Pealing loud as that of a cathedral bell,
Sounds fall short of the whizzing arrow of William Tell.

Frantic forest animals mate and date,
Before winter's wind, trumpets, deem them too late!
Nothing much can remain,
In such otherwise intense domain,
Except the breeze warm and balmy,
Soldiering evening's perfume strong and calming,

Summer, oh summer! I couldn't live without your sweet song of psalm,
Nor feel your tender kiss o'er my palm,
I wait patiently for you to be reborn.
Summer, my summer,
My redeemer,
Long forlorn.

Thoughts

Thoughts of earth's scent after the rain,
Thoughts of worries, pain and strain,
Thoughts powerful, to dine in hearts of pure beauty;
Let the ugly ones swiftly depart with no sense of duty.

Entertain thoughts wrapped in mystery,
Those that need no formula for chemistry.
Let white rain fall upon parched thirsty soul;
To quench thoughts appears not bold.

Brave thoughts that will not wither,
But commands embrace with delightful quiver.
Thoughts filled with nature in simple awe and wonder!
Orchestrated to music – not a far cry from rapturous thunder.

Thoughts of wild vine, flower, fruit, thorns entwine,
Never fail to adorn in bounties twisted in shape of a shrine,
Thoughts of white roses, dry days withstand,
Yet, falter not, or alter their place on motherland.

Thoughts of honeysuckle shifting stubborn sod,
Clearing a way among thick tight shrub, nothing odd,
Air filled with stifling, pungent, untamed whiff of honey,
Bees undeniable faithful grub, not at all funny.

Thoughts of your victories make you quiver,
Thoughts of the glories they deliver.
Oh! thoughts of love, oh! how it rocks your core,
Thoughts of a heart forlorn, albeit not too torn or worn.

Thoughts of moments seize, cherish,
Thoughts of the dog-gone years perish,
Pitched-high laughter of dear friends, such divinity of sound will never end.
But cling to the clavicle of your chest – not bend.

Thoughts of unsavoury promises,
Ones that inevitably must go amiss,
Thoughts of another, cast burden on oneself,
Heave them high on a dusty shelf.

Ah yes! clothe thoughts in constant sunshine,
Equally in rare rainbows, dare not to draw the line.
Let thoughts go far and wide afield, let them grow:
Feast upon them as if it's your last day tomorrow.

Time

Your shortness of presence, like a dandelion's bouquet often amazes,
Flying and diving in such pace of frantic wild praise,
Burrowing deep and falsely lead in a sweet polonaise,
Looped in the tick-tock of a clock in a divine maze,
With no unfolding clear design, its prey coyly slays.

A lark resounds with its faraway lonely cry,
Cannot master you, dare but try;
Boundaries withstand, adhere with a subtle reply.
Time masters few, disappearing like summer's last butterfly,
There your secret lies, far above the sky.

Like sand quickly washes ashore, bask in softness then go,
Leaving behind a feeling, a place for desire to grow,
Like melting ice, drips slow, slow, slow and then fall below,
As a fountain spray its droplets and weeps at its toe,
Dancing steadily, then disappears without a glow.
Fly on, fly on, drift on, drift on my time, surely amidst conflict,
Take your mighty wings, crack them like bursting flames in a fire-pit hit,
Then change laughter into a frown, I must admit,
Your cracked face in a net of wrinkles none omit,
Soon light in eyes leaves a dull memory trace, a heart must quit.

Waterfall

Steady beads of narrow tears transcending,
With valour and chaos you fall,
Casting ruin, in steady awaiting pool below,
A maze of cool transparent beauty shows,
These are glorious things!

The hollow sound, echoes meet and greet the senses,
Falling below like the tone of a lonely oboe
Belting sheets of spray, no end,
In the shadow sings its fiery volley,

A quieting tempest, torments wrapped in white spray,
Quiets the mind, yet plagues and sings to the heart,
No fear or pity, crave none in the slightest,
Then a cowardly peace follows,
Lost in a vision that enchants and soothes.

Wild

Wild birds do sing,
The call of the cuckoo clings,
The skylark with its silver wings,
Soars off to far lands, such a thing!

Wildflowers cock their heads in a haughty way,
With petals swaggering, competing in their display.
Busy buzzing bees hang about all day,
Willing to feast and suck nectar lay.

Trees swaying tall and proud,
Gosh! the wind is so loud,
While tall corn mounts higher on earth's ground,
Weeds grow low, with fierce frowns on brow.

Lazy stream gurgles, my oh my!
Seems to sing a soothing lullaby.
The hovering dragonfly rushes by,
No care, no fear, not even a sigh.

Thick knitted grass, no easy pass,
A very tedious task for the grasshopper swishing by last,
Not even for the cricket with its high-pitched note sounding cast,
Wild, yes you, your heaven with all creatures vast,
Thank you for creating such a blast!!

A Winter's Noon

The bucolic spirit was drunk with heavy vapour,
Time unaltered, in presence ever steadfast;
The damp late winter presses in non-resisting helpless noon air.
The lingering fine tune brook babbles and gurgles,
Emitting an adagio, constant, seductive like a Babylonian symphony,
Breaking through entrenched roots in dark wet earth,
Controlled by time, ageing-parade no sign of cumbersomeness.
Crescendo, ripple, harp, twigs, decaying leaves with hint of colour once was,
Transport upon surface in a slight mad rush.
Masters of the forest bare sculptured torso strong, rough nude,
Stood tall and poised like the ancient Greek god "Kratos".
Leafless branches with long limbs stretch menacingly in mid-air.
Embedded roots suffocating, wrapped by delicate green moss,
And woven by clinging to determined ivy.
Winter bush grows sparse, scraggy yet youthful,
Flaunting its peerage of vibrant yellow, bell-like foliage, among leafless allies beneath heel.
The sky bleeds a lofty drizzle,
Instantly, vegetation, open space – without hesitation,
As apostles in bowing reverence.
Heeded the nearby pond, a bevy of trumpeting swans, quacking ducks,
Saturated, pierced, sabotages the otherwise stillness
Of the thick cool mist-defeated silence,
Stretches its nameless excellence into subordination
To the loud noise, with ease and swagger.
Enchanted by the sublimity of the high noon, I jolted,
Ears pricked to the deniable crunching noise underfoot.
Clear path lay forth, I was home again.